How expressing your praise to God enhances your relationship with Him

7 DAY DEVOTIONAL

ANDREW HOPKINS

Copyright © 2020 Andrew Hopkins

All rights reserved. This book or any portion thereof may not be reproduced or used in any manner without the express written permission of the publisher except for the use of brief quotations in a book review.

Unless otherwise noted, Scripture taken from the New King James Version®. Copyright © 1982 by Thomas Nelson. Used by permission. All rights reserved.

Scripture quotations marked NIV are taken from the Holy Bible, New International Version®, NIV®. Copyright © 1973, 1978, 1984, 2011 by Biblica, Inc.™ Used by permission of Zondervan. All rights reserved worldwide - www.zondervan.com. The "NIV" and "New International Version" are trademarks registered in the United States Patent and Trademark Office by Biblica, Inc.™

Published by Breaker Ministries
ISBN: 978-1-7351430-0-2
ISBN eBook: 978-1-7351430-1-9

CONTENTS

Introduction 1

DAY 1
IT'S ACTUALLY NATURAL 3

DAY 2
SECRET PLACE VICTORY 7

DAY 3
LORD OF THE DANCE 11

DAY 4
USE YOUR HANDS 15

DAY 5
HUMBLE YOURSELF 19

DAY 6
CRY OUT! 23

DAY 7
OVERFLOW OF THE HEART 27

Conclusion 33

INTRODUCTION

God is raising up passionate, expressive, and intimate worshippers in this hour. He longs for His church to be fully engaged in relationship with Him. Praise and worship is meant to be a wholehearted expression and God is more than worth all the affection of our hearts! The truth is, when our hearts get touched, it makes its way to outward expression (see Matt. 12:34b).

It's been said, "If you do what you've always done, you'll get what you've always got." I've found, specifically in the area of outwardly expressing praise & worship, the Lord wants to push people out of what they've always done so they can discover Him in a fresh way. He wants to release a greater level of encounter in your life but it's going to take a greater response from you. He wants to expand your expression and give you a fresh encounter!

The Lord has put it in my heart to equip the church to be well-rounded worshippers who love His Presence and respond accordingly.

Let's praise Him with all we've got!

DAY 1:
IT'S ACTUALLY NATURAL

*"Great is the Lord, and greatly to be praised;
And His greatness is unsearchable."
Psalm 145:3*

When I first got saved I had one of my mentors tell me a dream he had when he was first discovering God. Simply put, he had been praying for 3 weeks straight next to his bedside asking God to reveal Himself to him. Then, in a dream, he was taken to heaven. The Lord spoke things to him and he encountered the presence of God. Yet, one of the things that stood out to me was when he woke up, he was sitting upon his bed with his hands lifted and praising God! He didn't know anything about the "how-to" of praise & worship or the lifting of hands - it just came naturally!

Here's the truth - outward expression in praise & worship isn't a charismatic or pentecostal thing - it's a human being thing! Not only that, it's a Bible thing and a God thing! (Check out Ps. 47:1, 40:3, 84:2, 95:6, 149:3 for references to shouting, clapping, singing, crying out, kneeling, and dancing). All the expressions of praise & worship you see in the Bible can also be found in many other non-Christian arenas. They are natural to human beings because God created us to be expressive - just like He is!

Someone could say that it's just not their personality to be expressive, but the reality is, if you have enough reason to, you would naturally burst forth with a shout of excitement, lift your hands in victory, or even cry with sheer joy! As a side note, emotions are also part of the package of being made in God's image. Obviously we want to be submitted to Holy Spirit and not let our emotions lead us, but at the end of the day, emotions can be super helpful in expressing our love for God. The bottom line is this - Jesus' worth and work is enough of a reason to celebrate for all eternity!

Here's the challenge: we get comfortable in the familiar. It happened to the people of Jesus' hometown of Nazareth. As Jesus was teaching in the synagogue the people got offended. They said, "Is this not the carpenter, the Son of Mary, and brother of James, Joses, Judas, and Simon? And are not His sisters here with us?" So they were

DAY 1: It's Actually Natural

offended at Him." (Mark 6:3). In other words, they couldn't get past the Jesus they grew up with! Just because they grew up with Him didn't mean they knew all there is to know! It's like how Bobby Conner says, "We've become far too familiar with a God we barely know."

Because of this, the story goes on to say that Jesus couldn't do a mighty work there (Mark 6:5). Notice it didn't say wouldn't, it said couldn't. "Would" has to do with "will" but "could" has to do with "ability." The Son of God was actually limited because of familiarity! God wanted to do more in Nazareth but the people weren't able to get past who they knew Jesus to be. In other words, God wanted to expand their view of Jesus, but they had to participate with the process. We have to break familiarity with the Jesus we think we know!

In regards to praise & worship, many of us become comfortable in what's easy for us. But God wants to do a mighty work in your life. I believe if you step out and do something you've never done before, God will meet you there and do something in you that you've never experienced before. You'll experience Him in a fresh way.

Someone might say, "It's really about the heart and the outward expressions are more optional."

EXPAND YOUR EXPRESSION

Try telling that to your wife or husband! I say, yes, it's about the heart and if your heart really gets impacted, then it will make its way to the outside.

1 John 4:19 says "We love Him because He first loved us." The foundation of all worship is responding to God's initiation. His love and worth revealed to us empowers us to worship with all our hearts - to give Him back what He first gave us. Jesus said that those who've been forgiven much, love much (Luke 7:47). Take a moment to think upon His cross, the price He paid for you, the love He shows you, and the vastness of His worth and identity.

Questions to ponder:

- What are some expressions you see outside the church that parallel biblical expressions of praise?
- As you consider the outward expressions prescribed in the psalms (sing, shout, dance, kneel, lift hands, etc), which ones are you comfortable with? Which ones are challenging to you?
- Can you see yourself breaking into more freedom in expressing praise to God?

DAY 2:
SECRET PLACE VICTORY

"But you, when you pray, go into your room, and when you have shut your door, pray to your Father who is in the secret place; and your Father who sees in secret will reward you openly."
Matthew 6:6

Several years ago, I came back from a highly impactful worship conference (which you will hear more about tomorrow) and I received so much breakthrough in the area of dancing my praise to the Lord. Every morning I would get up, turn up the high praise music, and dance! I would celebrate like crazy. I'd be jumping on the bed, spinning around, laughing, and just plain out having a blast with the Lord.

There was so much freedom and joy!

Yet for some reason, as I would be foolishly celebrating before the Lord, I would look over my shoulder, embarrassed, as if someone was there seeing my wild dance party. But I was actually in my room, the door shut, the blinds closed, and no one was around! Nobody was there to be embarrassed in front of! I was getting embarrassed for myself!

I eventually stopped caring and just kept on praising; which brings me to my point - if you can get over yourself in private, then you'll have more confidence to be free in public! Ed Cole said it like this: "Your private practice determines your public performance." And ultimately, Jesus said that the Father rewards you openly for what you do secretly. There's a victory to be won in the secret place. It's in the secret place of devotion where we develop deep and intimate worship as well as exuberant and high praise. As a side note, I believe there are also breakthroughs to be had in corporate settings of praise & worship that you can't get alone. But this secret place devotion is crucial to becoming a well-rounded worshipper. It's where the depth of your heart is developed.

Proverbs 29:25 (NIV) says, "Fear of man will prove to be a snare, but whoever trusts in the Lord is kept safe." One of the greatest things holding people back from being expressive in praise and worship is the fear of man. In other words, we care too much about what people think. It's the over-thinking that actually snares us. It holds us back from our full potential. We must overcome it!

DAY 2: Secret Place Victory

We can care too much about what people think in at least two extremes. One, we hold back our expression because we don't want people to see us or hear us fully give our praise to God. It can feel embarrassing because they are seeing a more vulnerable part of your life. Secondly, we can go the other way and want people to notice us exuberantly giving praise to God, because after all, we want people to know how free we are and would love their affirmation. In other words, we're trying to prove ourselves to them. We want to avoid these two extremes.

True worship is unto the Lord not man! It's not about being noticed by people, it's about honoring God and entering His presence! We need to refocus and center our attention on our great and mighty God! Your hunger for Him has to be greater than your care of what others think.

David said that it was before the Lord that he danced with all his might (2 Sam. 6:21). This is where the secret place comes in. It's there you learn how to minister unto the Lord without the distractions. You discover the pleasure of His presence. You get caught up in the wonder of His grace. You get transformed in the weight of His glory. And before long, expression becomes your normal because you won the secret place victory. Then, wherever you go, you're free to express your love for God because you've cultivated it and developed personal depth in the secret place.

I'd also like to challenge you to spend money on praise & worship music. Jesus said, "For where your treasure is, there your heart will be also." (Matt. 6:21). Your heart is connected to wherever you put your money. When you purchase a worship album, you're already engaging your heart in the worship journey. Then you're equipped to have radical encounters through praise & worship in the secret place!

Questions to ponder:

- Describe what the saying "Your private practice determines your public performance" means to you in regards to praise & worship.
- What extreme of the fear of man do you tend towards?
- What does your secret place time look like? Are there any adjustments you could make to go to greater levels of freedom and devotion?

DAY 3:
LORD OF THE DANCE

"Let them praise His name with the dance…"
Psalm 149:3

Several years ago, I went to a worship conference at Christ For the Nations Institute (CFNI) in Dallas, Texas. The keynote speaker opened up the conference with a message entitled "Lord of the Dance." He spoke how the world had, in some ways, distorted the original design for dancing and prophesied that the Lord was bringing the dance back to the church.

As a response to the word, he had the worship team lead us in an extended time of praise - specifically in the area of dancing! Imagine a full sanctuary of people jumping, leaping, and all the most awkward dance moves you can conjure up, and then do that for 30 minutes straight - all in direct praise to our awesome God!

There was such a level of freedom and breakthrough in the atmosphere it literally

EXPAND YOUR EXPRESSION

transformed my life. I was sore for days after that. But something got inside my spirit and has never left. It was the freedom to celebrate Jesus unashamedly.

This is what happened when David took over the kingdom of Israel and brought the ark of the covenant to Jerusalem. The Bible says he danced before the Lord with all his might! (2 Sam. 6:14). And when he was criticized (by his own wife!) for his dancing, he replied that he would become even more undignified! (2 Sam. 6:22). This was one guy who cared less about the opinions of people and highly valued his relationship with the Lord!

The root word in Hebrew for "hallelujah" (praise the Lord) is halal. It means to boast, to be clamorously foolish, to rave, to celebrate, to praise, to shine, and even act like a madman. So in actuality, "hallelujah" is a pretty exuberant word!

In my experience, many people rarely make it to this kind of praise. We like to stay generally mild in our expression. But there's one thing that needs to be sacrificed in order to access this kind of praise - your dignity! Jesus is definitely worthy of it all! The Apostle Paul even writes from jail,

DAY 3: Lord of the Dance

"Rejoice in the Lord always. Again I will say, rejoice!" (Phil. 4:4).

Someone could say, "Well, isn't that distracting or drawing too much attention to yourself?" The question is already focused too much on self. The question really is, will you give God your highest praise?

I love the life of revivalist and general of the faith, Smith Wigglesworth. He was recorded as saying, "I don't ever ask Smith Wigglesworth how he feels! …[in the morning] I jump out of bed! I dance before the Lord for at least 10 to 12 minutes – high speed dancing. I jump up and down and run around my room telling God how great He is, how wonderful He is, how glad I am to be associated with Him, and to be His child." And how great God used this man!

Just in case you were wondering, God is actually a dancing God!

Zephaniah 3:17 tells how He rejoices over His people. One of the Hebrew words for "rejoice" in that verse literally means to spin around with intense motion and leap for joy! In the New Testament, the Father was so overjoyed when the prodigal son came home, the scripture said you could hear music and dancing (Luke 15:25). Not only does God dance, but He invites you to get up off your seat and dance with Him in exuberant praise!

I would like to mention that I'm not saying we have to dance wildly every single time we praise God. But if we never venture into this kind of praise, then we're missing out on something God has for us (and has asked us to do!). Take a moment in the secret place and dance before the Lord with all your might! You won't regret it.

Questions to ponder:

- Have you ever danced with all your might before the Lord? What was that experience like for you? If not, imagine what a greater level of freedom would feel like.
- On a scale of 1 to 10 (10 being the most expressive), where is your level of freedom in regards to dancing before the Lord?
- What do you think you could do to push yourself to the next level of expression?

DAY 4:
USE YOUR HANDS

"Lift up your hands in the sanctuary, And bless the Lord."
Psalm 134:2

"Oh, clap your hands, all you peoples!"
Psalm 47:1

I remember the first time I began to lift my hands to the Lord. I didn't grow up in church and I really didn't know much about anything. So when I got saved at 17, I went to youth groups and just learned from what everyone else was doing. I honestly was kind of embarrassed for the people who were praising - smiling and clapping their hands...and even lifting their hands. I didn't understand what was happening until I experienced God for myself and had a reason to praise!

Once, in a time of worship, I just opened my hands, closed my eyes, and sang to the Lord. Again, I was just opening my hands because I thought if this what you're supposed to do, then I gotta do it! As I began to worship with open hands, this tingling sensation began coming on my hands. Now, I heard about the Presence of God, but no one told me what I was supposed to feel. This had never happened before in my life. It was especially meaningful to me because I had been asking God to show me that He was real.

Fast forward a few weeks or so, and there was a conference happening nearby that had some amazing worship leaders coming to it. Since I was a Christian now and these guys had good voices, I thought it'd be a good idea. The preacher at the service had an altar call, I came forward, and began to worship. This time I just went for it with all that I had. I lifted my hands all the way and sang to the Lord with all my heart. That same tingling sensation came again - yet this time, starting in the tips of my fingers, and went through my whole body. It was like liquid electricity. I believe that was when I was baptized in the Holy Spirit (Acts 1:8). All of this as a result of worshipping God with lifted hands!

I believe God has encounters waiting for you as you lift your hands in praise & worship to Him. Ultimately it's to honor Him and give Him your praise, but God responds to heartfelt worship.

The lifting of the hands can mean many things - surrender, victory, reaching out to the

DAY 4: Use Your Hands

Lord, open-hearted worship, casting cares on the Lord, etc. Worship is a relational thing and must be treated as so. The meaning comes from the context of your relationship with God. Even more, sometimes we don't even fully understand the why, yet we do it anyway out of learning, or obedience to the word, or the stirring of the Spirit. I've had moments where someone leading worship touches the heart of God, the anointing hits strong and I spontaneously just lift my hands in an almost involuntary response. I encourage you, even in the unknown, to lift your hands and bless the Lord!

In addition to lifting your hands, the scripture also tells us to clap our hands! At minimum, clapping your hands is a way to celebrate and show your approval and admiration for someone or something. In some cases, clapping hands helps the rhythm of the music - but if you don't have rhythm it could get weird (haha). In a deeper sense, applauding God with your hands brings breakthrough to an environment when done appropriately. It's part of making a joyful noise to the Lord and praise changes the atmosphere. It also promotes unity when the people of God clap together.

If you're happy and you know it...clap your hands!

EXPAND YOUR EXPRESSION

QUESTIONS TO PONDER:

- What is your experience with lifting your hands to the Lord? What has it meant to you?
- What are more reasons for lifting your hands that aren't named here?
- Do you think you could be stretched in the area of using your hands in praise & worship?

DAY 5:
HUMBLE YOURSELF

*"Exalt the Lord our God,
And worship at His footstool–He is holy "
Psalm 99:5*

Years ago, we had a guest worship leader at our church come and do a few Sunday services - two in the morning and then a special worship night. The morning services were great, but something so powerful happened at night. As we entered into a deeper time of worship, it was like the fear of the Lord combined with an awareness of His massive greatness entered the room. I remember kneeling in worship, bowing low to the ground, and wanting to go even lower if possible. It was like I couldn't get low enough. The King was so high and lifted up in that place that I could only think of going lower.

It seems in this hour the Lord is bringing to His church the powerful revelation of sonship. What a beautiful thing it is to be the sons and daughters of a mighty God, to be heirs of God and co-heirs with Christ, and to be able to call Him "Papa" or "Daddy"! Yet in the midst of it all, we can't lose the revelation that our God is also the holy King of Glory who reigns supreme. He is massive and beyond comprehension. All rulers, authorities, principalities, and powers are all subject to Him. From everlasting to everlasting He is God. It's this revelation of God that calls us to humble ourselves before Him - kneeling, bowing, and even prostrating ourselves.

Remember, the Apostle John was the one who was found leaning up against the chest of Jesus at the Lord's supper (John 13:23). What a posture of intimacy! Yet years later, he has an encounter with the Lord that left him on the ground as though he was dead! (Rev. 1:17). What made the difference? He saw the risen Christ in all of His glory. The King made Himself known to him.

There are times to dance, clap, and celebrate the Lord - but there are also times to humble ourselves before the King. It's another area where you sacrifice your dignity for the Lord. It's a posture of complete submission and humility. In fact, a Hebrew word commonly translated as "worship" in the scripture means to bow down, and even prostrate yourself. (see Ps. 95:6).

DAY 5: Humble Yourself

What a healthy thing to be reminded that you are not God! You are not the sole provider, the savior, the healer, the restorer, the king, etc. When you bow before Him, you are showing your utter dependence upon Him. It's a posture of seeking Him in humility. It re-aligns your heart. Even the elders in heaven fall down before the Lord and worship Him! (Rev. 4:10)

I would also like to make mention that you can also humble yourself and at the same time be in a place of intimacy and even gratefulness. We see this happening in the scriptures.

> *"...Mary, who sat at the Lord's feet listening to what he said." (Luke 10:39 NIV)*

> *"He threw himself at Jesus' feet and thanked him..." (Luke 17:16 NIV)*

Mary sat at Jesus' feet in submission and listened to His words. The one leper out of ten who got healed came back, fell down at Jesus' feet, and gave Him thanks. What a beautiful place to be when at the feet of Jesus.

QUESTIONS TO PONDER:

- When is the last time you humbled yourself before the Lord? Is it time for a fresh surrender?

EXPAND YOUR EXPRESSION

- Are there any other reasons you can find for humbling yourself before the Lord?
- What are the benefits of worshipping God like this?

DAY 6:
CRY OUT!

*"My soul longs, yes, even faints
For the courts of the Lord;
My heart and my flesh cry out for the living God."
Psalm 84:2*

I was at CFNI another time as they were hosting a Friday night worship night. In the middle of a worship song the Lord spoke to my heart and said, "I want you to cry out to Me." Mind you, this wasn't at the end of a song where the cymbals were crashing, everyone was clapping and the music came to a crescendo where my voice could hide in all the noise. This was in the middle of the song!

So I let out a little measly and pitiful yelp.

The Lord spoke again, "I want you to cry out to Me!" So after my awkward half-hearted yelps, I just let go and went for it, crying out to God with full heart and voice. Again, such a level of breakthrough and freedom happened in that moment that it never left me! I experienced the

EXPAND YOUR EXPRESSION

Presence of God in such a powerful and fresh way.

I had actually experienced this type of crying out in prayer meetings and the secret place, and even when I was leading worship. But to just cry out and let my heart express what it needed to express in public like that was still nerve-wracking for me. I love how the Lord leads us past our insecurities!

There's something about the shout and the raising of your voice to cry out that breaks barriers. We can see even in the story of defeating Jericho, the people of Israel shouted and God wrought a great victory (Josh. 6:20). The raising of your voice requires full physical engagement. You can't be passive and cry out to the Lord! In other words, it pushes you past the threshold of passivity and into passion! It breaks the passive barrier and causes you to fully engage. It gives expression to the deep desires of your heart.

I remember hearing some well-known worship leaders saying the reason why they put songs in such high keys is so that people would have to really raise their voices in order to hit the notes! I love that!

The scripture talks about raising our voices in a shout of triumph (Ps. 47:1), shout of joy

DAY 6: Cry Out!

(Ps. 100:1), high praise, and to express hunger and desperation. The story of Blind Bartimaeus (who isn't blind anymore!) illustrates this crying out powerfully (Mark 10:46-52). He heard that Jesus was coming by and began to cry out for his healing. People told him to be quiet but instead of calming down, he cried out all the more! The bible says that Jesus actually stood still in response to the crying out, and then commanded Bart to come - and he received his healing!

It was the raw hunger and desperation in the heart of Bart that caused Jesus to stop in His tracks and release healing and breakthrough! Bart realized that there's something in Jesus that meets a need in himself - so he cried out! Our need for God has to be more important than our inconvenience and religious customs. Sometimes the best way to express your hunger is to cry out. Like the Psalmist said, "My heart and my flesh cry out for the living God." When is the last time you cried out to God? He wants to release breakthrough in your life!

Furthermore, when is the last time you gave the Lord a shout of praise? As a worship leader I joke around with the people I lead because when I lead them to lift up a shout, most of the room claps their hands. I usually jokingly say something like, "Do your hands have mouths? Let's use our

EXPAND YOUR EXPRESSION

voices and lift up a shout!" Again, it makes you have to engage when you lift up your voice. It's the threshold we've gotta cross!

> *"Make a joyful shout to the Lord, all you lands!" (Ps. 100:1)*

Questions to ponder:

- Think of a time you really cried out to God. How impactful was that for you and how did it help express what you wanted to say to God?
- What are other reasons you can see for lifting up your voice?
- Are there any barriers in your life that could use a shout of victory or cry of hunger to bring breakthrough?

DAY 7:
OVERFLOW OF THE HEART

"...be filled with the Spirit, speaking to one another in psalms and hymns and spiritual songs, singing and making melody in your heart to the Lord, giving thanks always..."
Ephesians 5:18-20

It's day 7! I trust that there's been breakthrough in your life as you've expanded your expression to the Lord and praised Him with all your heart! My hope is that you use the teachings here as springboards into greater encounters with the Lord.

I want to conclude this series with an encouragement to sing your own songs!

Years ago, worship leader Rita Springer came out with a song called "All I Need." Singing about the profound simplicity of just needing to worship the Lord and be in His Presence, the song is so full of intimacy and overflow of love. I was just giving it a listen for the second, or maybe third time in my office, and my heart just exploded with love for Jesus and His Presence. I honestly couldn't do much except for weep and let my heart be satisfied with Him.

Not only did the entire song carry such a sweet intimacy, there was a part in it that she led the people in spontaneous praise and worship. She encouraged the people to sing their own song to the Lord and just worship Him. On the recording you could hear the people lifting up their voice in genuine adoration of the King. God was so present in my office as I worshipped Him. I had to stop everything I was doing and be in His Presence. Why?

Psalm 22:3 tells us that God sits enthroned on praise. He makes a dwelling place there. The Hebrew word for praise in Psalm 22:3 is tehillah. It means the new song, the spontaneous song, the overflow of the heart. It's this kind of praise that attracts the Lord to come and make a dwelling place in. That's why I was having such an encounter!

Going even further, if this kind of praise makes a throne for God, then that means His Kingdom power is present because kings sit on thrones. If His Kingdom power is present, then it's an atmosphere for miracles, breakthroughs, joy, freedom, deliverance, and victory over the enemy!

DAY 7: Overflow of the Heart

In the New Testament, the Apostle Paul encourages us to sing spiritual songs to the Lord. It's the New Testament counterpart to tehillah. The spiritual songs are the songs birthed by the Spirit. Coming from the deep and core part of who we are, we sing the overflow of our hearts to the Lord. It's beyond the written song. It's the overflow of gratitude, honor, love, and intimacy.

Sometimes the songs are in our native language, and many times in our spiritual language. Paul would also write, "...I will sing with the spirit, and I will also sing with the understanding" (1 Cor. 14:15). When we sing in line with the Spirit, we are doing what Jesus said is true worship (John 4:23-24). Spirit to spirit communication. Deep intimacy with the Father.

I encourage you to break out of the norm and sing a new song to the Lord! Whatever you're grateful for, whatever you love about the Lord - sing it in praise to Him. Sing hallelujah! And when you run out of words, just sing in tongues and let your spirit commune with His! It's some of the deepest form of communication. (If you don't speak in tongues yet, ask Him for it! It's a gift He wants to give you! See Mark 16:17).

I've seen corporate worship times go to a whole new level of Presence when the people engage in this kind of worship. What's happening is an entire room is engaging in some of the deepest forms of worship at the same time and the collective hunger and passion in the room creates such a powerful landing place for the Lord to move. You move beyond just what you can comprehend in your mind to the deeper things of the Spirit.

This kind of worship is one of the keys to accessing the deeper things of the Spirit. We are first spiritual people and not mere men and women (1 Cor. 3:1-3). We are partakers of the divine nature and the Spirit of God lives in us. You were made for this! I believe God wants to take you into deeper levels of encounter with Him as you worship in this manner. Go for it!

Questions to ponder:

- Have you fully engaged in this type of praise? How did it impact your time with the Lord? If you haven't, why not start now?
- Out of all the expressions discussed in this devotional, which ones do you feel the Lord leading you to dive deeper into?

DAY 7: Overflow of the Heart

- After these 7 days, why do you think it's important to outwardly express your praise and worship to the Lord?

EXPAND YOUR EXPRESSION

CONCLUSION

It's time to give God the glory He deserves! Give Him all your praise! Give Him all your worship! I want to pray for you:

Lord Jesus,

I pray for all those reading this devotional. Lord, release a breakthrough in their lives as they give You praise. Let this be a catalyst for deeper relationship and encounters with You. I pray for sweet times of intimacy and powerful times of victory. Most of all, I pray Your Presence comes so strong in their times with You that beyond what these teachings say, Your Spirit would teach them how to worship. Thank You, Lord.

Amen!

CONCLUSION

ABOUT THE AUTHOR

Andrew Hopkins is a prophetic worship leader, revelatory preacher and teacher, and moves in the supernatural. He worked at his local church for over a decade in various pastoral positions and currently heads up his own itinerate ministry, Breaker Ministries. He also works at Elisha Revolution, with Jerame & Miranda Nelson as Worship Director and Associate Revivalist. Andrew earned a Bachelor degree in Christian Studies in worship from Vision International University. He and his beautiful wife Rochelle have two boys, Hunter and Everett, and live in San Diego, CA.

BREAKERMINISTRIES.COM

BREAKER MINISTRIES

@BREAKERMINISTRIES

ALSO BY **ANDREW HOPKINS**

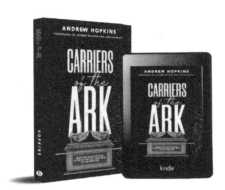

CARRIERS OF THE ARK

"Andrew takes you on a journey of hosting the Holy Spirit and spreading Kingdom impact as you hunger for more of God in your life."

- **Ché Ahn**, Founder and President, Harvest International Ministry

The world around you needs God's Presence and you were created to carry Him!

This book is a training manual on what God wants to form *in you* so you can carry more of Him *upon you*!

We are the modern-day **Carriers of the Ark!**

GET YOUR COPY TODAY AT amazon.com

SEND OUT YOUR ROAR EP

8 original songs that are sure to provoke passion for Jesus, stir up the Spirit of revival, and release encounter with the God of the Breakthrough.

AVAILABLE AT:
breakerministries.com
& all online music stores

Made in the USA
Columbia, SC
20 November 2024

47007521R00029